G000269663

STREETS OF LONDON TRANSPORT

Mick Webber

Capital Transport

Front cover A bustling Whitechapel High Street at Gardiners Corner looking towards London in the 1930s. This part of what was a Roman road from Colchester to London, and now is part of the A11. There was a strong Jewish presence in the area at this time, and many of the shops and market stalls in vicinity were run by the Jewish community. The famous Petticoat Lane market was and still is just to the north. Aldgate East Underground station opened here in 1884. Many bus and tram routes served this road, and among many others, we can identify TD 40 on the left on route 25C and STL 859 on the right on the 42 to Finsbury Park. In the line of tramcars heading for the Aldgate terminus are two ex-West Ham vehicles. Nearest the camera car 303 is inbound from Ilford on service 63. It follows an ex-Leyton E3 on route 61. On the outbound track is a standard ex- LCC E1 vehicle working the 'round the houses' route 71 to Aldersgate. The church in the background is St Botolph without Aldgate, built between 1741 and 1744. *London Transport Museum*

First published 2017

ISBN 978-1-85414-418-8

Published by Capital Transport Publishing Ltd
www.capitaltransport.com

Printed by Parksons Graphics

Title page Tottenham Court Road south of Goodge Street station in the early 1950s. RT family buses abound.

Above Oxford Street on a sunny day in 1957. Stockwell's RTL 1265 is on the 2A and shares the street with other RT family buses, including a Green Line relief. An RF on route 715 is flanked by two taxis. The big store on the right is C and A, the big clothing chain that was once present on many high streets. *Vintage Images*

Opposite This very rare second world war shot of LTs lined up in Park Lane is taken from a film still, hence its lack of sharpness. The line-up is of buses between the peaks that are needed for peak hour work and will begin their evening duty from here rather than returning to their garages and using valuable petrol in the process. Similar lines of parked buses were to be seen elsewhere in London also.

INTRODUCTION

When the idea of a London street scenes book of London Transport vehicles from 1933-1969 was first mentioned, I didn't need my arm twisting. When you get the chance to trawl your photo collection of buses, trams and trolleybuses, and pick out favourites that hopefully haven't been seen before, you have to say yes!

We have tried to represent the suburbs of as many parts of London as possible, as well as the central area. The photos show how much the capital has changed in many areas, and some historical notes have been included to hopefully add interest to the scenes. The backgrounds in these images show a world long gone, with once famous High Street names in view, and vehicles once commonplace.

The important part that electric traction once played in the capital is portrayed, with the overhead wires and tramlines that were once an everyday sight. I am grateful to the photographers that have let me use their work, and apologise to anyone that has not been credited.

I would like to thank Robert Harley for his work on the tram captions and the help given by Jim Whiting throughout this project. Chris Holland and Peter White read through the captions and supplied very useful comments and corrections. Finally, encouragement from Peter Horner and Robin Newell and Margaret McNicoll, as always, pushed me on.

Mick Webber, Blackheath 2017

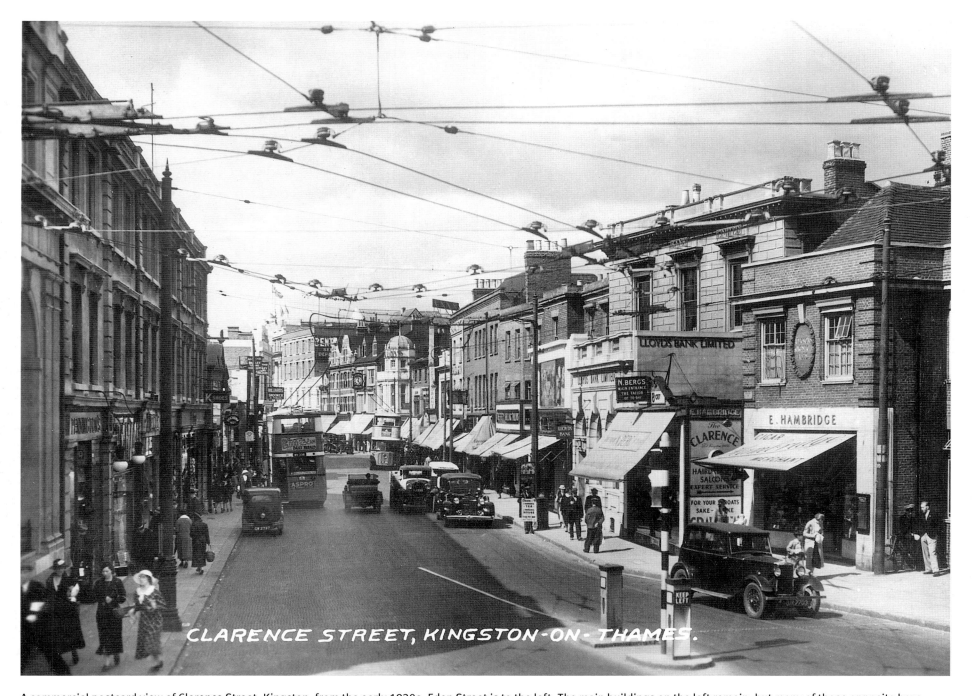

CLARENCE STREET, KINGSTON-ON-THAMES.

A commercial postcard view of Clarence Street, Kingston, from the early 1930s, Eden Street is to the left. The main buildings on the left remain, but many of those opposite have now gone, and this is now a pedestrian area. In July 1933, London Transport assumed control, along with many other companies, of London United Tramways. With their fleet came a batch of sixty trolleybuses known as 'Diddlers', which had been introduced very successfully in May 1931. Two of these can be seen here and the one facing is on route 4 to Wimbledon. The route was later renumbered 604, and in May 1962 was the last route operated by a London trolleybus.

Merton bus garage was opened by the London General Omnibus Company in November 1913. This is the scene on 28th May 1937 when services resumed after a strike. The police are in attendance to ensure all goes smoothly as STLs 836 and 707 leave to take up service on routes 77 and 88. Merton shared the allocation of the 77 with Chalk Farm and the 88 with Sutton and Shepherds Bush. The maximum vehicle requirement for the garage was 208 buses on Monday to Friday. The drivers are wearing their summer white coats in accordance with the rules. *Topfoto*

Single deck LTs 1175 and 1097 have terminated at Edgware Station in the 1930s. These LTs (internally referred to as LTLs) were 2ft 7ins longer than the double deck LT and, at 29ft 5ins, were the longest buses in the fleet at the time. The Northern Line was extended to Edgware from Hendon in August 1924 and was eventually planned to run on to Elstree with a new depot at Aldenham. After the war, the plan was abandoned and the new depot became the Aldenham Bus Overhaul Works.

Muswell Hill Broadway in the mid-nineteen thirties. LT 1023 is one of two of the class terminating here. These AEC single deckers were built by the LGOC in 1931. The scene here has changed very little over the years, and buses still terminate here. The buildings on the Broadway, which stretches off to the top left, are all still here. United Dairies, which occupies the building in the centre, is yet another once familiar name to have disappeared.

St Georges Circus, Southwark, was built in 1771, and was one of the first purpose built traffic junctions in London. There was originally an obelisk here, but in 1905 it was relocated to ground in front of the Imperial War Museum. A clock tower was built in its place, and is seen in this 1930 view. This didn't last long, and was demolished in the 1930s as "a nuisance to traffic". The Royal Eye Hospital was located here in 1892, and became a section hospital with beds for servicemen with eye injuries during the first war. It was badly damaged in the second war and had to be closed in 1941. It reopened in 1944 and became part of the NHS in 1948. Closure came in 1980, and it was later demolished. This view is late 1933, and London Transport has yet to display the new fleet name on its inherited vehicles. Ex-LCC tram 1032 on the left, is bound for the Embankment, whilst STL 253 is travelling south to Croydon. The bus on the right bound for Finsbury Park is NS 169. Note the tramways pointsman on the left, just behind the ornate cast iron tram stop. *Getty Images*

Herne Hill on 20th June 1935, with Dulwich Road off to the left and Herne Hill and Half Moon Lane straight on. The scene has changed little today, the building occupied by Jones the Tobacconists remains along with the buildings just visible beyond the bridge. The station here was opened in 1862 by the London Chatham and Dover Railway, initially to Victoria and later to Farringdon Street. The Thameslink service now calls here. NS 886 is turning right into Dulwich Road on the 37. When this class of bus first appeared in 1923, they were open topped, had solid tyres, and no glass windscreen. By the time they entered their final year in 1937, these omissions had all changed. This vehicle was built in November 1923 and withdrawn in May 1936. The other bus is STL 25, a March 1933 built vehicle which is about to travel the length of Herne Hill and Denmark Hill. *London Transport Museum*

Belsize Road, Kilburn on 25th June 1935. The Kilburn Palace on the left was originally the Town Hall built in the 1880s. It was modified as a theatre and called the Theatre Royal and in 1900, under new ownership, it was renamed the Kilburn Theatre of Varieties. Gaumont took over in 1930, and after closure as a theatre in 1940, it became a night club in 1953, and later a warehouse. The auditorium has now been demolished, but the frontage is partly intact but under threat. Kilburn High Road station is behind the wall on the right, opening in 1852. NS 238 is working the 31 to Chelsea, having just passed a sister vehicle working to Camden Town. It is obviously straw hat weather judging by the man outside the cinema. On the right of the bus, a man on a motorbike appears to be asking for directions. *London Transport Museum*

Opposite It is a lovely sunny day at the approach to London Bridge station. The date is 24th April 1935 and, judging by the heavy coats worn by the ladies on the left, there is a chill in the air. They could, of course, go in to the Lyons corner house for a cup of tea. The white and gold front of the famous tea shops spread all over London from their first in 1894 in Piccadilly until there were over 250 in the capital. Nothing is forever, and they all came to an abrupt end in 1978 when Allied Breweries had their takeover offer accepted. The bridge carries the line to Charing Cross and Cannon Street. Emerging into the sun is ST 17, a February 1930 bus built at Chiswick. It will terminate here and rest before its 99 minute return trip to Harrow Weald. *London Transport Museum*

George Street, Richmond on 10th May 1935. NS 1948 passes Rego Clothes and Barratts shoe shops on the right, in buildings that remain. The opposite corner has been redeveloped. The 37 was a main trunk route across south London between Hounslow in the west, and Peckham in the east. In recent years, the route has been cut back from Hounslow to Putney. The bus would continue to give service until November 1947. The flags are out to celebrate King George V Silver Jubilee. *London Transport Museum*

Opposite top Looking towards the High Street in Teddington. The town was historically in Middlesex until 1965, when it became part of the new London Borough of Richmond upon Thames. When London Transport decided to replace its trams with trolleybuses it built two new vehicles, a four-wheeler and a six-wheeler, to enable them to choose which would be the more suitable for the future fleet. The six-wheel vehicle, which was the eventual winner, was numbered 62 and can be seen here at the terminus of route 5 outside the Savoy cinema. The route was soon to be renumbered 605. The film 'One night of love' was released in 1934, when this vehicle was built. The building seen here, was replaced by a bigger cinema in 1937 but the site was redeveloped in 1960. *Richard Stevenson Collection*

Opposite Proof positive that London's tramways were not only confined to inner city areas. Here on the Uxbridge Road by the Red Lion Hillingdon there is almost a village atmosphere, enhanced by the splendid seventeenth century church of St John the Baptist. A touch of modernity is added by the presence of ex-London United tramways car 2137, one of the Feltham or UCC batch of vehicles intended to bring 'luxury' travel to regular passengers on route 7 from Uxbridge to Shepherds Bush. In the background construction work is proceeding on a new dual carriageway road. This redevelopment doomed the tramway and trolleybuses took over on 15th November 1936. *London Transport Museum*

Children from Dulwich Central School are taking a traffic census as part of their geography lesson on the local area. It is Forest Hill Road, and the date is 21st January 1938. The three boys and their teacher seem more interested in the camera than the traffic, but at least four of the other five appear to be taking notes. One of the early 'Fire call' alarms is mounted on the pavement. The bus on route 63 is STL 512, which was new in July 1934, and is operating from Chalk Farm garage. Just visible on the right is Charringtons, the coal merchant. The universal fuels for home heating in those days were wood and coal, the latter delivered in one hundredweight sacks to basement cellars in homes all over London. *Topfoto*

A double deck LT has just started its 68-minute journey to Stratford Broadway as it turns into Oakleigh Road North on route 34 at Whetstone. The single decker is LT 1054 on route 251 on its way from Arnos Grove to Burnt Oak. The shop on the left and the others beyond still exist, although the corner property is now a café. The buildings on the right have all gone, and the road is substantially wider now, forming part of a big junction with the Great North Road and Totteridge Lane. The year is 1935. On the right is a very typical newsagent's shopfront of the time and placards are in good supply. *London Transport Museum*

Opposite London Transport began to instal roadside shelters early in 1934, most of which were designed by Charles Holden and the first being erected at Shannon Corner, Malden. The one shown here is outside Queensborough Court on the North Circular Road in Finchley, where an experimental Bus Stop design was also tried out as one of a series of designs that led to the adoption of the red circle and white-lettered black bar version that soon after was adopted as standard for compulsory stops and remained so for about 40 years. *London Transport Museum*

This variation on the same theme was installed at Fair Cross, a short distance from Barking bus garage, which can just be seen on the right and on the other side of the road. Its elegance is in sharp contrast to the aluminium Q shelters of the early post-war years .
London Transport Museum

In addition to the standard designs, other types of shelter were produced to suit varying conditions. For rural locations timber construction was sometimes used, and for places where the pavement was too narrow to accommodate the design above, this canopy type was installed.
It provided limited protection from the elements but gave plenty of space for maps and timetables at busy locations. This example is seen outside Green Park. *London Transport Museum*

Richmond Road in Kingston on 10th May 1935. Residents of the town had a wealth of cinemas to visit. Three can be seen in this picture. On the right is the Empire, built in 1910, converted to offices and a supermarket in 1956, and then partly a pub. Much of it remains today. Nothing else in this view exists now. The cinema on the extreme left is the Kinema, opened in 1910 and closed in 1983, and the one in the centre is the Elite, which operated from 1921 until closure as the Century in 1955. The site was later occupied by a C&A store. Just beyond the Kinema, and out of view, is Kingston bus station and garage. STL 736 is about to enter and stand before returning to Mitcham on the 152. Once again, the flags are celebrating the Silver Jubilee of George V. *London Transport Museum*

The junction of Bromley Road with Sangley Road, on the right, at Rushey Green. The first three buildings on the right have now gone, but the next three remain. The tower on the right in the distance is on the roof of the 'Black Horse and Harrow' pub, which is also still in situ. The stone fronted building on the left was opened in 1932 as the Concert Hall, and is now a grade II listed building. Pulling out of Sangley Road and crossing the conduit tram tracks, is STL 77, a January 1933 bus with bodywork built by Thomas Tilling. LT 845 waits at the kerb on the left on training duties, whilst an STL on the 137 bound for Highgate, picks up passengers. A retrievable pulley-operated electric lamp hangs over the middle of the road. *London Transport Museum*

Streatham Common is ancient common land where tenants could graze their cattle. The Black Prince granted the common to Christs Church Canterbury in 1362, and it later passed to the Ecclesiastical Commissioners in 1862. The Metropolitan Board of Works purchased the land from them in 1884, in order that it should be used as a public place, and it has been that way ever since. The common is on the right in this view, with the Greyhound pub just out of sight on the left in Greyhound Lane. A single deck LT on route 234 is just emerging on the left from Greyhound Lane. LT 892, built in December 1931 by the LGOC, is on route 49, and will turn short here before heading back to Shepherds Bush. Note the elaborate street lamp on the island on the left, bearing the pub sign. The year is 1935. *London Transport Museum*

In November 1935, London Transport unveiled an attempt to streamline one of its fleet. STL 857 was modified and rebuilt with a full front and sloped front profile. The bus was renumbered STF 1, and entered service from Tottenham on route 73. Within a short time, it was moved to Hackney where it worked on the 6. A rare view is shown here as it makes its way into the Marble Arch gyratory. The experiment came to an end after overhaul in 1937, when it reverted to STL 857 with a traditional half-cab arrangement, although the sloped profile remained. *Capital Transport Collection*

Nominally part of the former Leyton fleet, car 197 was originally stationed at Bow depot. Here it is seen outside the Green Man Leytonstone. Although repainted in LT livery, it has yet to receive the London Transport house style Johnston numbers but retains its attractive LCC type fleet numerals. These E3 class vehicles were regular performers on trunk route 61 Aldgate to Bakers Arms, until the route was converted to trolleybuses on 5th November 1939. *London Transport Museum*

A very busy Hammersmith Broadway at the junction with Queen Street in the mid-thirties. The impressive Portland stone frontage of Hammersmith station is associated with the extension of the Piccadilly line from 1932, and this entrance was opened in 1934. It was demolished in 1988. The Green Line coach is T 395, built in 1930, originally owned by East Surrey, and fitted with an opening canvas roof. This area was transformed in 1960 when work began on the Hammersmith flyover which was built to take the main A4 traffic. *London Transport Museum*

Opposite top Old Bond Street in the 1930s. The very grand Royal Arcade is on the left. It was built in 1879, and links Old Bond Street with Albemarle Street. The word 'Royal' was added to the name after H.W. Brettell, a shirt maker and one of the Arcade's first occupants, was patronised by Queen Victoria. The bus is LT 1394, built in 1932, and is one of the class known as 'Bluebird' after the interior colour scheme of the buses when new. The bodywork was built by the LGOC at Chiswick. One could be forgiven for assuming that the street was one way at first glance, owing to the spread of vehicles facing the camera. It was not, however, and drivers proceeding in the opposite direction would have to weave their way through. *Richard Stevenson Collection*

Opposite The Strand in the early 1930s. Architect John Nash redeveloped this western end of the Strand in the 1830s, and the street was well known for theatres. Many of these have now gone with only the Adelphi, the Vaudeville and the Savoy remaining. In the centre of this view is the Tivoli, a theatre and cinema built in 1923 on the site of a previous theatre which had been demolished in 1916. Sadly, this one was closed in 1956 and offices now occupy the site. Two STLs are travelling east followed by four taxis, and the bus approaching is ST 202, built by the LGOC in June 1930. A Rolls-Royce waits outside the Tivoli. *London Transport Museum*

The tube came to Golders Green in June 1907 as the Charing Cross, Euston and Hampstead Railway. Extensions to Hendon in 1923 and Edgware in 1924 followed. The substantial station buildings on the right provided passengers with shelter whilst waiting for their London trains. A large forecourt was provided for the linking bus and coach services. A variety of vehicles can be seen here, including NS, ST, STL, single deck LT, and T type coaches. In the background on the Finchley Road, a trolleybus heads north. The buildings here remain and the substantial Midland Bank in the centre still gives services to its customers. The buses here now face the opposite direction. *London Transport Museum*

Opposite Victoria station forecourt in 1938/39. The standard London buses of the pre-war years are all here. From left to right are all-Leyland STD 70 new in May 1937, LGOC bodied ST 728 from February 1931, LPTB bodied STLs 1944 and 2435 from May and December 1937, and LGOC built LT 1286 new in April 1932. Victoria has always been one of London's main bus terminal points from the London General days, and their inspector's tower to the left now bears the LT bullseye. Victoria was the terminus for the London, Brighton and South Coast Railway, and also the London, Chatham and Dover Railway, and it opened in 1860. The buildings in this view all still exist except the control tower and mess block on the lower right. *London Transport Museum*

Car 1191 slows to a halt on Westminster Bridge Road opposite the entrance to Lambeth North tube station. The motorman applies the handbrake as a pedestrian hurries in front of his tramcar. On the left of the picture a tram in Kennington Road is about to join the tracks to Westminster Bridge and the Victoria Embankment. In October 1935 standard E1 class car 1191 was included in the London Transport 'rehab' scheme for modernising some of its fleet. Allocated to New Cross depot, the vehicle was withdrawn in September 1950. It is 9th June 1935. *London Transport Museum*

Opposite top Sutton station was opened by the London, Brighton and South Coast Railway in May 1847. It now handles about seven million passengers a year and provides a direct link with London Victoria and via the Thameslink service to St Pancras and beyond. T 134 is a 1930 LGOC built coach which is working route J, a half hourly service scheduled to take 141 minutes from end to end. Originally in the County of Surrey, Sutton has been a London borough since 1965. *London Transport Museum*

Opposite Aldgate on 7th April 1937. The bus and coach station here was cramped and overcrowded. The east London Green Line routes X, Y1, Y2, Z1 and Z2 provided links to Romford, Brentwood, Corbets Tey, Tilbury and Grays. In addition to this, short turning buses also had to be accommodated. When the conversion from trams to trolleybuses was in progress, it would mean turning points for the new vehicles would also have to be found when the Commercial Road and Mile End tram routes were replaced. In this view it appears that work had already commenced to cover the District and Circle line tracks with a platform to facilitate a larger bus station. The two Green Line coaches are T 298 and T 94. The bus on the right is Upton Park's TD 104, which has terminated on the 25, and distant is STL 327 on the 15. Note the two heavy duty buffers of the left designed to stop terminating trains coming into contact with District Line trains. *London Transport Museum*

26

This is the Edgware Road looking south in 1935. The bus is NS 27, a vehicle built in 1923 and which lasted until 1937. It is about to turn right and stand on the forecourt of the Crown public house. The LGOC had used this point as a terminal for its horse buses from the 1880s and London Transport was to continue its use until the late 1960s. The original 18th century building was replaced by the present structure in 1889. The large terrace on the right is happily still with us, but the buildings on the immediate left with the adverts have been demolished, and the Crown hotel now occupies the plot. *London Transport Museum*

Opposite top Woolwich Road looking west on 10th May 1935. The bus is about to turn right into Westcombe Hill, and will travel through Blackheath, Lewisham, Catford and Sydenham before arriving at the Crystal Palace, which was destroyed by fire in November the following year. The bus is NS 2214, and is one of thirty specially designed vehicles for operation through the Thames tunnels. The roof profile differed from the standard NS, and apart from one experiment, all kept their solid tyres. When the first of these started work in April 1927, they were the first buses in London to have enclosed staircases. The street lights here were on a pulley, and could be pulled across to the side for maintenance. A hundred yards further on was the entrance to the Charlton tram overhaul works. *London Transport Museum*

Opposite The East End in the mid-1930s. We are looking down St Paul's Road, since renamed St Paul's Way, towards the main railway line to Fenchurch Street. Nothing except the railway bridge is left of this bygone scene of east London. Bowles the family butcher's delivery bike is on the left, and the first standard telephone kiosk type K1 is just behind, with the post box near the kerb. Corner shops were dotted around most back streets, and three can be seen here. The bus is STL 16, a 1933 vehicle, working to Poplar on the 106. Tram route 77 passed here at this junction with Burdett Road. *London Transport Museum*

The Elephant & Castle intersection had been a major transport hub since horse tram days. Here in the early years of the London Transport regime, traffic congestion was becoming a serious headache. At first sight this scene resembles organised chaos as trams, buses, lorries and private cars vie for road space. In London Road a lone horse and cart has appeared behind an 84 tram outbound for Peckham Rye. To the right of the picture in Newington Causeway the motorman of a tram on route 6 and the driver of the 35 bus wait patiently for the traffic policeman to give them the right of way. *London Transport Museum*

At Vauxhall we look north from Wandsworth Road into the Albert Embankment. Just beyond the two Kings Cross bound buses and the two tramcars, the tracks turn left towards Vauxhall Bridge. Car 457 on route 12 heads for the Borough, Hop Exchange terminus. This E class vehicle dates to 1906 and was still giving sterling service some three decades later. Car 552, approaching on its way to Wandsworth High Street, was a newer specimen, having been built in 1929/30. A gyratory traffic scheme was later introduced at this location. New tramlines were laid and the whole layout opened in April/May 1938. *London Transport Museum*

The scene is Aldgate tram terminus just on the edge of the City. London's tramways were not welcomed in the streets of the square mile, which remained the preserve of the motor bus. Note that a loading island has been provided for intending passengers. Car 936 on route 63 to Ilford was one of the first batch of modernised, rehabilitated trams, being so treated in July 1935. It was allocated to Bow depot. The following vehicle is an ex-Leyton E3 on service 61. The date is 9th March 1936. The country's ruling monarch since January has been Edward VIII, but he would not be at the end of the year and was never crowned following his decision to give up his right to the throne so that he could marry an American divorcee. *London Transport Museum*

An elegant lady attired in a coney fur coat looks towards the camera. Note the wickerwork baskets full of shopping – no plastic bags in those days! It is 10th February 1939 and war clouds are looming, despite prime minister Neville Chamberlain's proclamation of 'peace for our time' the previous November. On the day before this photograph was taken the Home Office had announced that thousands of British homes in areas most likely to be bombed in the event of war would be supplied with corrugated iron for 6ft 6ins by 4ft 6ins air raid shelters of a design that could be built by two men without the need for any special skills. Tram service 55 was replaced by trolleybuses on 11th June 1939.
London Transport Museum

It is Whit Monday, 29th May 1939. The scene is the Royal Forest Hotel in Rangers Road, Chingford, and the crowds are patiently waiting to board their buses after a day out in Epping Forest. Three STL type buses are working the 145 and 102 routes. The 38 and 205 also started from here. One wonders when looking at the faces of some of these people whether they had any idea of the events that would take place in the following September. *London Transport Museum*

The Crown and Castle pub in Kingsland Road Hackney. This Victorian pub dates from 1851, and served beer and spirits until 2005, when it was closed and converted to a restaurant. The K class trolleybus on route 677, is leaving Balls Pond Road, and will cross the junction into Dalston Lane on its way to Smithfield. It is a sunny day in Wartime, and the shadows of the overhead wires can be seen on the roadway. The trolleybuses have had their front mudguards painted white to aid visibility in the blackout, but do not appear to have had their headlamp blackout masks fitted.

The first bridge at Waterloo was opened in 1817. It lasted until the 1930s, when, after years of problems with settlement, it was decided to demolish it. In the interim period, a temporary bridge was constructed, which can be seen on the left. The new bridge construction was completed during the war and partially opened in March 1942. The full opening occurred in September, and STL 2496 is heading north on the 67, followed by an ST. Only one pathway for pedestrians is open at this stage, as shown in this American press photograph. *Mick Webber Collection*

This is the main Whitechapel Road looking east at the junction with Cambridge Heath Road on the left in November 1940. The trolleybus is N1 class No 1609 on the 663, which had been introduced on the 5th of that month to replace tram route 63. The Green Line coach on route Y2 is T 715 working to Hornchurch. Coming towards the camera after the cyclist are two firemen on a motorbike, and on the right is a man – possibly a window cleaner – pushing a hand cart with a ladder. *Mick Webber Collection*

Opposite Chaos at Gardiners Corner, Aldgate. A German daylight bombing raid on 19th September 1940 caused this scene of devastation. The trolleybus is K1 class No 1122, which had been working the 647 when it was caught up in the blast, and has had all of its windows blown out. The overhead repair crews would have their work cut out to get all of the wiring back in place before service could be resumed. One of the signs outside the ladies hairdressers advertises 'shingling', which was a popular cropped haircut of the day. Note the conduit tram tracks. During the Blitz in this part of London, these were still serviceable, but were never used again after the trolleybus conversion programme. *Getty*

The scene is Aldgate bus and coach station, and the date 22nd February 1941. A welcome brew-up for the crews is supplied by the mobile canteen that London Transport have installed. The conversion programme from tram to trolleybus has been suspended due to the hostilities, and would not be resumed after the war. The five drivers are joined by two clippies and an inspector. After the 57 continuous days of the London Blitz the previous year, the cheerful looking staff here are among Londoners enjoying a period of relative quiet. Hitler's Luftwaffe had turned its attention to other British cities. In February, Swansea came under three days of intense attack aimed at its docks and oil refineries. *London Transport Museum.*

The scene is Swinton Street, Kings Cross on the last day of 1947. The driver of trolleybus No 952 class J1, has lost control on the icy road and dewired. Bamboo poles are being used to rectify the matter and, with any luck, the vehicle will soon be on its way to Holborn. A woman from an upstairs window surveys the situation. Trolleybuses had replaced trams here in March 1938, and they in turn would lose out to buses in November 1961. *Topfoto*

This is North End Croydon in the late 1940s. Most of the buildings here have now gone, and much is now pedestrianised in this area. The bus is STL 1007 working route 411, which ran from West Croydon to Reigate. Trams on routes 16, 18 and 42 are still operating at this point, and will continue to do so until April 1951. STL 1007 will continue in service until April 1953. Richard Stevenson Collection

Opposite On 16th October 1948, Spurs entertained Queens Park Rangers in a Division Two match at White Hart Lane. They won 1-0. The 69,719 supporters streamed out of the ground, and many into the main Tottenham High Road to travel home. The trolleybus was their main form of transport here, and the orderly formed queues are supervised by inspectors and policemen. On route 649 is K3 class No 1672, an October 1940 vehicle working from Edmonton depot. *London Transport Museum*

All the fun of the circus! Six elephants from Bertram Mill's circus taking part in a drive to encourage the public to invest in National Savings. "If you don't need it, don't buy it" was the slogan in a Britain still in post-war rationing mode. It is 5th May 1948, and the crowds are out in force in Ilford High Road. The trolleybus held up in all of this is one of the forty-three originally destined for delivery to South Africa. Due to the dangers to shipping during the war, it was agreed that they would be diverted to London, where vehicles were needed to replace war-time losses. The 693 was operated by Ilford depot, where all of these non-standard vehicles were stationed. *Topfoto*

It is 8th June 1950, and it should be a nice early summer's day. Instead, a heavy thunderstorm has hit north London with localised flooding, and in Edmonton the wooden setts in the road have lifted. The children are out, possibly collecting the blocks, which were very good for the fire. A row of trolleybuses can be seen in the distance, and K2 class No 1192 gingerly makes its way through on its way to Waltham Cross. The local shop on the right advertises 'Vesta Marvo distemper', a water-based wall colouring that was very cheap and easy to apply in the days before washable paint was available. *Getty Images*

The Blackwall Tunnel was opened in 1897 by the Prince of Wales, soon to be King Edward VII. It was designed by Sir Alexander Binnie and work began in 1892, the total cost being £1.4m. Seven deaths were recorded during its construction. The twentieth century traffic problems soon made it clear that a second tunnel was needed, and work commenced in 1960, the second tunnel being opened in 1967. In this view, tram 134 is on route 58, which terminated here. It is a former LCC HR2 class car built in 1931, designed for hilly routes, and was one of the 101-159 batch delivered without trolley poles. The bus is STL 1868 working from Athol Street garage on route 108A. The buses operating through the Thames tunnels were of a different design to the standard STL, having a specially contoured upper deck profile to suit operation through the Blackwall and Rotherhithe tunnels. Forty were built in 1937, and all operated from Athol Street garage. *Geoff Morant*

Opposite This view is looking east along the Strand with Waterloo Bridge off to the right. The church in view is St Mary-le-Strand. The original church here was demolished in 1548, and the replacement we see here not built until 1723. Pre-war buses from the STL and STD classes are in view, as well as some RT family buses from the post-war era, most of which still have the wartime destination blind restrictions in evidence. The once very welcome Lyons tea shop is seen in the centre with its traditional white and gold paintwork. Note the sign in the centre foreground for 'Trams', directing people towards Waterloo Bridge, where passengers could descend the steps to the Embankment below for services to south London. It will not do so for much longer, as this photo is from 1951 and the subway will close the following year. *Getty Images*

This commercial view of Morden station forecourt was taken between March 1949 and March 1950. The Northern line was extended here in September 1926, and a busy bus terminus has been located here ever since. The bus on the far right is D 125, a utility Daimler with Park Royal bodywork delivered in July 1945. The bus in the centre is one of 190 loaned from the British Transport Commission, delivered new to London Transport from Eastern Coach Works before going on to their eventual new owners. They all arrived in the liveries of their destined fleets. This particular one was numbered MB899 in the Hants and Dorset fleet and was a Bristol K6A. It worked from Merton garage from March 1949 until March 1950.
Richard Stevenson Collection

The market town of Romford is an extremely busy shopping area. This view of South Street confirms the fact and there are ten buses here, all challenging for road space. RT buses predominate. The bus on the left is an Eastern National Bristol KSW5G on the 2A to Southend, fleet number 1423, which was once with Westcliffe-on-Sea. Note the National Provincial Bank on the left before it merged with the Westminster to become the Nat West.
Richard Stevenson Collection

Woolwich Powis Street was the main shopping area in the town. It is named after the Powis brothers, who were Greenwich brewers who took out a lease on the fields here in the eighteenth century. In this scene the distant towers of the Royal Co-operative Society buildings can be seen on both sides of the road, and the Co-op had a huge presence in the area until 1985. The two buses here are from the batch loaned to London Transport when new and before delivery to their eventual owners. Both are destined for the Crosville fleet. On the left is MB323, and on the right MB321, both Bristol K6As. They were in service at Plumstead garage from January 1949 to April 1950 and from December 1948 and March 1950 respectively. *Richard Stevenson Collection*

London Transport was allocated 281 utility Daimler buses which were delivered in 1944 and 1945. D 93 was a 1945 delivery with bodywork by Brush of Loughborough, and lasted until September 1953. The camera has caught it here on a wet day in the Strand on route 77. The Whitbread lorry is a Dennis 50cwt 'flying pig', which is followed by a Ford 'Y' type van. *Charles Klapper*

The photographer stands outside St Leonard's Church, Shoreditch to record the approach of car 1915, which is working Kingsway Subway service 31. An ominous sign for the future of tramway operation at this location is the appearance of the new trolleybus overhead wires. Something has distracted the tram driver, as he edges his charge forwards across the road junction in the direction of Hackney Road. This peaceful scene of summer 1939 would soon be shattered by world events and the outbreak of the Second World War. *London Transport Museum*

Opposite Woolwich, Beresford Square on 17th October 1951. The square, named after General William Beresford, master of the Royal Ordnance, was formed in the early 19th century. The Woolwich Arsenal itself had been an armaments manufacturing site from the late 17th century, ceasing this work in 1967 and being vacated by the Ministry of Defence in 1994. The main gatehouse, built in 1828, is to the left, and the square is bordered by market stalls to the left and right. Working from Old Kent Road garage, RT 4095 is on its way to Plumstead Common on route 53A. Two trams are on the right, the one nearest the camera on the 46 will pass through Eltham and Lewisham on its way to New Cross Gate. A distant trolleybus on the right is on the 698, and a London Transport breakdown lorry waits to the right of the trams. The track curve off to the left was installed in 1944 to enable cars to travel from the Eltham area to the factories in Charlton and was paid for by the Ministry of War Transport. *Topfoto*

Car 2003, on its way north of the Thames to Manor House, turns out of Brixton Water Lane on to Effra Road. In order to reach its objective this vehicle will traverse the Kingsway Subway. It is accompanied by RT 1939, which is working route 3. The scene is unchanged today, with the Victorian terrace all intact. The pub 'The George Canning' off to the left, still exists, although by another name. Trams worked a one-way loop here, northbound via Water Lane and southbound via Morval Road. Among Brixton's claims to fame are Electric Avenue, one of the first shopping arcades with electric lighting, and Charlie Chaplin, who was once a resident. *LCC Tramways Trust*

Pedestrians cross behind tram 167 in Upper Street Islington, near the Angel. Tram routes 31, 33 and 35 shared this busy stretch of road with trolleybus routes 581, 609, 677 and 679 and no fewer than 11 bus routes. Two members of the RT family are in view and these will very soon take over from the trams. The demographic of Islington has changed substantially since this photo was taken, along with skyrocketing property prices. In 1952 the average price of a London home was £2,650, which today would buy you a fairly old second hand car. An average flat in Islington will set you back over £600,000. *Don Thompson, LCC Tramways Trust*

A total of 100 type UCC Feltham cars entered service with the London United Tramways and Metropolitan Electric Tramways companies. After being incorporated into the LPTB fleet they were ousted from their original routes by trolleybuses. Here in south London, they found a second home. Car 2128 (ex LUT car 359) is caught on camera in Streatham. It is working the long route 18 from the Victoria Embankment to Purley. The Felthams were destined for further use in Leeds after their sojourn in London was over. Two young spotters appear to be taking an interest in the tram.
LCC Tramways Trust

A dull miserable day in the Holloway Road in the early fifties. Tram 1944 is a former LCC E3 car built in 1930, and will shortly terminate at Highgate. Trolleybus overhead dominates the sky as we look south at the Nags Head junction. The pub after which the area is known, first opened here in 1851, and continued until closure in 2004. The building remains. Tram route 35 was one of three routes to operate through the Kingsway Subway, the others being 31 and 33, all operated by Holloway depot with help from Wandsworth, Norwood and Camberwell.

Electric traction is out in force at Woolwich, Beresford Square in July 1952. Class E3 car 1911 on route 40 is within yards of its terminus at Woolwich, Perrott Street and the conductor has already changed the rear indicator blind. It is last tram week, as can be seen by the side advertisement, and on 5th July 1952 they will cease to operate. The trolleybus on route 696 is working short to Bexleyheath, and is class D2B No 405B; the 'B' denoting that its original body was destroyed in 1944 and a replacement by East Lancs was fitted in 1946. The bus on the right is RT 1760 from Catford garage on the 75 and is about to turn right and head off for leafy Blackheath and all points to West Croydon. The main gate to the Woolwich Arsenal can be seen on the left.

In the forties and fifties, London was plagued with deadly smog, a thick poisonous, polluted fog, the worst of which descended on the capital in December 1952, and lasted for five days. Official figures state that about 4000 deaths could be directly attributed to this. The capital suffered from smog many more times until the clean air act of 1956 dramatically improved matters. Victoria station forecourt is the scene here, and RT family buses dominate on routes 25, 11, 16 and 38. The RT on the right is a Saunders bodied bus which was new in 1950. *Topfoto*

Old utility Daimlers on Green Line routes from the east into London, were replaced from July 1950 by new RTs. RT 3233 is on the 722 at Stratford bound for Aldgate with the yellow on green destination blinds. This bus was delivered in July 1950 to Romford, London Road garage, and stayed until its first overhaul in November 1954. It remained a Romford bus until 1963. The pub on the right is the old Black Bull, opened in 1829, and is the only building in this view that still remains. *C.Carter/London Transport Museum*

RTW 274 has fought its way through the traffic from Kensal Rise, and has reached Piccadilly Circus. It still shows the wartime restricted destination display and its original livery with the cream window surrounds. The graceful curve of Regent Street is behind, headed by the splendour of the County Fire Office, which was completed in 1924. The bus displays adverts for the weekly magazine 'Everybody's' which along with others such as 'Picture Post' and 'John Bull', kept people occupied in their front rooms in the days before the mass invasion of television. *Vintage Images*

Shoppers from Eltham disembark from car 92 at the last stop before the terminus in Beresford Square, Woolwich. Many of them will have realised that this is the final day of tramway operation in London – Saturday, 5th July 1952. Next week they will have to get the bus. The days of post-war austerity are almost over; this is the start of more prosperous times, which have no place for the tramcar. The range of wares available in the Sidney Ross shop were advertised as children's clothes, cots, playpens, pushchairs and 'Really Exciting Toys'. In this chain of shops, those of the 'baby boomer' generation took their first steps. *F.E.J. Ward, Online Transport Archive*

Whitehall c.1951. The name was taken from the Palace of Whitehall, home of the Monarchs from Henry VIII to William III, before it was burnt down in 1698. Many Government buildings are located here, including the War Office building, which is seen here with the two towers. The work done here was transferred to the Ministry of Defence in 1964, and although it continued to be used, it was sold off in 2014. The centre piece, however, is the Cenotaph, erected in 1920 replacing a temporary wooden structure, built to commemorate the dead of the first war, and used as a memorial to the fallen from all conflicts ever since. The bus on the right is utility Daimler D38 working on route 88. *Vintage Images*

Park Lane was originally known as Tyburn Lane, after the village of the same name, and was later the site of the Tyburn gallows, London's main public place of execution until the late eighteenth century. It was a main thoroughfare in the twentieth century, and traffic was reaching saturation point in the 1950s. Between 1960 and 1963, it was made into a dual carriageway by claiming some 20 acres of Hyde Park to complete the work. An underground car park was also constructed at this time. In this view in the early 1950s, traffic is at a standstill southbound. An STL and an RT family vehicle are in view at a time when the use of cream paint around the upper deck windows was being discontinued.

Decorations are in place for the 1953 Coronation. The road here at the south end of Whitehall assumes the name of Parliament Street. Apart from the STL travelling north on the far side, all vehicles are of the RT family. The bus in the centre next to the Austin lorry and on route 11 is RTW 325, closely followed by a sister vehicle on the same route. All buses here still have the restricted blind displays, despite good progress having been made by this time on the reintroduction of full displays. *Best Impressions*

On 2nd June 1953, the nation celebrated the Queen's Coronation. The capital was decked out with decorations and people flocked to see the build-up to the big day and the illuminations at night. All bus and coach routes normally entering the main area of the Coronation route were curtailed at temporary turning points and London Transport issued a special map with all of the details for the travelling public. It also ran special evening services for sightseers. This view of Oxford Street captures the array of colour, with Selfridges centre stage. Two STL type buses and two RT family types are seen, together with two of the twenty-five RF private hire coaches in their smart green and grey livery. The weather wasn't so kind on the big day; it rained. *Vintage Images*

Piccadilly Circus was laid out in 1819, when Regent Street was being built under the supervision of John Nash. In the centre is the Shaftesbury Memorial, which was erected in 1893, and is surmounted by a statue of Anteros. In this view we can see the Coronation decorations on the main buildings and on the curve of Regent Street, with an elaborate gold centrepiece over the memorial. RT family buses dominate here, the last ones not being delivered until the following year. *Alamy*

At Trafalgar Square some of the Coronation decorations are in place, barriers have been located, and staging is being erected around the base of Nelson's Column. Apart from the STD in the bottom left, all buses are of the RT family. On Coronation day, 2nd June 1953, the route will pass here on the way to Westminster Abbey from Buckingham Palace. It will then pass again on its way back from the Abbey, on route for Piccadilly, Park Lane, Oxford Street and Regent Street, and then a third time before returning to the Palace via The Mall.
Alamy

Regent Street in 1960. The RT family by now have dominance in central London. The Routemaster is beginning to emerge, but has yet to make an impact in the centre of the capital. Also dominant in London is the Austin FX3 taxi, several of which can be seen in this view. It was made between 1948 and 1958 by Carbodies of Coventry. The car nearest the camera is a Ford Consul. Dickins and Jones, on the right, had a presence in Regent Street since 1919, although at that time it was owned by Harrods. Its subsequent owners had kept the name, but the store eventually closed in January 2006. *Alamy*

The trams have gone and now RT family buses predominate, as seen here with an RT leading an RTL along the Victoria Embankment. Sir Joseph William Bazalgette was the man behind the building of the Embankment, which conceals storm relief and waste pipes to take the main sewage away from London. What is now the District and Circle lines of the Underground, also occupy the area beneath the roadway. Building work began in 1864, and the area was opened to pedestrians in 1868, with the roadway being unveiled in 1870. *Julian Thompson*

South End, Croydon in the mid-fifties. RT 2950 from Elmers End garage works the 194 to Croydon Airport. The airport was first used in 1915, and enjoyed expansion in the 1920s and 30s. It was closed to civil aviation during the war, but reopened in 1946. Closure was decided in 1952 and it eventually came in September 1959. The Westminster Bank building on the left still stands, although it is no longer a bank, but the corner building on the right has been replaced. All other buildings still remain. Note the RAC sign on the right for Croydon Aerodrome, which closed at the end of September 1959. *Julian Thompson*

The Royal Exchange in the City of London was opened in October 1844, although the original building here dated from 1571. Built as a "centre of commerce", today it is a luxury shopping and dining area. It has Threadneedle Street to the left and Cornhill to the right, and in between is RTW 312 on its way to Alperton from Old Ford, on the Sunday only route 8B. The adverts on the bus are for a vermouth made in Kingston that is still produced today. *Julian Thompson*

The site of the West London air terminal in Cromwell Road is now Sainsbury's, Gloucester Road. It was once a thriving hub for BEA passengers and this temporary structure built in 1957 was later replaced by a much larger building. Passengers checked in here for their flights and were then transported to London Airport (as it then was) by a fleet of specially built coaches. They were based on the AEC chassis used for the RF class, but had Park Royal one-and-a-half deck bodies with a large luggage area beneath the upper half deck. MLL715 was delivered in 1952 and was one of 65 built. They were phased out in 1966 and 1967 to be replaced by specially adapted Routemasters. These coaches were owned by BEA but operated by London Transport. The check in facilities closed here in January 1974. *Julian Thompson*

With Selfridges famous store in the background, RTW 486 travels west along Oxford Street followed by another of the class on the same route. Route 6B, which began on 29th January 1964, was unusual in being introduced with a mixed RTW/RM allocation as it replaced RTW route 6 and RM route 257 on Saturdays. It became mixed RM and RML in October 1966 until its withdrawal in September 1968 as part of the massive changes in north and north-east London that saw the start of London Transport's bus reshaping plan published two years earlier. *Alan B. Cross*

Eltham High Street has changed very little over the years, and these buildings are all still in situ. The pub on the far left is the Rising Sun, once frequented by Jack May the actor who played Nelson Gabriel from the radio series 'The Archers'. Again we see once famous names of the past, the 1940 Cleaners, Lewis the tobacconists, and the Fifty Shilling Tailors. The latter once had nearly 400 shops across the country, it was founded in 1905, and was sold off in 1958, the new owner renaming it John Collier. It, in turn, was sold on to Burtons in 1985. RT 2696 was delivered in September 1951 with a Weymann body, and resided at Catford garage until August 1955. It will terminate at Welling, Guy Earl of Warwick, one of the many pub bus stands that once existed. *Fred Reynolds*

Bexleyheath clock tower, on the left, was unveiled on 11th July 1912 to commemorate the Coronation of King George V the previous year. In later years, it acted as a roundabout, and a convenient turning point for trolleybuses on routes 696 and 698. In this view on 2nd March 1959 the trolleybuses have just one more day to operate before being replaced by RT type buses. RT 433 from Plumstead garage works on route 122 and will terminate at Bexleyheath depot. The blind has already been set for the return trip to Woolwich. The poster on the right reminds us that 1959 was an election year. The Conservatives under Harold Macmillan won against Labour's Hugh Gaitskell. *Alan Cross*

It is October 1959 and the Motor Show has started at Earls Court. The surrounding streets are packed with traffic, as can be seen here on a dismal wet day. The bus is RTW 328 working from Battersea garage on route 31, a route shared with Chalk Farm. An interesting array of vehicles complete this street scene. In the foreground is an Austin/Morris J2 open van followed by an Austin A40 and a Rover. Behind them, are a group of lorries comprising a Ford Thames on the left, with a North Thames Gas Dennis Max at the rear. In the centre is a Bedford A type, and on the far left a British Road Services Albion. *Alamy*

On rare occasions, usually when Piccadilly was being resurfaced, buses have been diverted down the Mall and past Buckingham Palace. It is not known if her Majesty was at home at the time of this 1950s diversion, but perhaps Prince Phillip may have used his camera to record the event! Forest Gate's RT 1775 approaches the Palace on route 25, whilst Battersea's RTL 368 circles the Victoria Memorial on route 19. Note the Daimler ambulance passing the palace, once a very familiar sight in the capital. *Frank Mussett*

The Great Western Railway opened the original West Drayton station in June 1838 and it was relocated to the position as seen here in August 1884. T 762 was one of the post-war batch of the class and was delivered in September 1946 with bodywork built by Weymanns. This bus saw further service in Ceylon in January 1959. Route 222 started in Uxbridge, calling at London Airport on its way to Hounslow. Note the tiny shops on the right: a gents' hairdressers, a ladies' clothes shop and a grocer all in the space normally occupied by a single shop. *Norman Rayfield/2RT2 Group*

Holborn on 6th May 1961. The trolleybus is K2 class No 1205 dating from December 1938. It is on route 543 from Stamford Hill depot, and in July the route will cease to operate and be replaced by buses on route 243. The main building in the background is Gamages, a well-loved department store that will always be remembered by children for its wonderful toy department. It was founded in 1878 as a watch repair shop, and over the ensuing years, others properties alongside were purchased, until it reached the proportions we see here. They also operated a large mail order section. The store closed in 1972, and the area was redeveloped. *Peter Mitchell*

St James's Street Walthamstow. The trolleybus is M1 class 1548, which has travelled from Crooked Billet, and will pass through Leyton and West Ham on its way to the Docks. It is about to pass under a railway bridge at St James's station on the Liverpool Street line, which was originally the Great Eastern Railway. Behind is the Ashley House pub, on the corner of Blackhorse Road, and Braham's shoe shop occupies a corner site opposite the two ladies wearing their headscarves, very typical of the time, which is early 1960. Visible on the poles supporting the overhead are notices about stage 5 of the trolleybus to bus conversion; the 687 was to survive until stage 6. *Fred Ivey*

The Queen's building at Heathrow Airport was opened by Her Majesty in 1953, when it was renamed in her honour. It was originally known as the Eastern Apex Building. The viewing platform on the roof was a very popular venue for the public. It was demolished in October 2009 to make way for the new terminal 2. In this view on 2nd August 1964, Saunders RT 1795 leaves the Airport on its way to Mill Hill on route 140. Heath Row was a small village that was demolished to build the airport in 1944 and London Airport, as it was then known, was renamed Heathrow in 1966. *Norman Rayfield/2RT2 Group*

Opposite top Station Road, Wood Green. The railway bridge here carries the line to Palace Gates (for Alexandra Palace) and was opened in October 1878. Its losses proved unsustainable and it closed to passengers in January 1963. Road works force RF 491 on to the wrong side of the road as it leaves Wood Green behind on its way to Finsbury Park in this late fifties view. West Green garage was able to double deck the route after the bridge was removed. *Norman Rayfield/2RT2 Group*

Opposite The Classic cinema opened in Brighton Road, South Croydon in 1911 as the Swan Electric. It had several name changes before becoming the Classic in 1936. It closed in October 1973. Note the smartly dressed young man on the steps! It is 17th May 1964 and routes 190 and 59 will share the road as far as Coulsdon, where the 190 will turn left to Old Coulsdon and the 59 will run on to Chipstead Valley. Both buses are Saunders bodied RTs, the one in front being RT 4220 from Thornton Heath garage. *Norman Rayfield/2RT2 Group*

London Bridge station in the mid-fifties. London Bridge was London's first rail terminus when it was opened on 14th December 1836 and rebuilding in 1864 allowed trains to run on to Charing Cross, and in 1866 to Cannon Street. Substantial queues built up here for the buses to take people on into the city and beyond, and in this view RT family vehicles on routes 8A, 43 and 133 can be seen. RTW 461 is the bus on the 8A and, like many of its class, found further service in Ceylon in 1966. *London Transport Museum*

London Bridge station in the mid-sixties. The through trains to Charing Cross and Cannon Street use the branch to the left of this view, and on the far right is the terminal station, once in the ownership of the London, Brighton and South Coast Railway. The station is the fourth busiest in London. Most of the forecourt at this time, was still covered with cobblestones. The bus is RTL 1218, which is working on the 133 from Brixton garage; it was withdrawn in 1968. *Mick Webber Collection*

New Bond Street in about 1964. It is the northern half of the street, the southern section being known as Old Bond Street. The jewellers Bentley & Co on the right, now Bentley & Skinner, hold a Royal Warrant. RTL 458 on route 25 is the only one of six RT family buses identifiable in this view. It was at West Ham from 1962 to 1965, and in 1966 it was sold for service in South Africa. *London Transport Museum*

This is the junction of Blanche Lane with St Albans Road in South Mimms in 1968. St Giles church, parts of which date back to the 13th century, is to the right, and the White Hart pub, which is also a listed building, is on the left. Wood Green's RT 4263 with a Park Royal body, has just started its long journey to Victoria on route 29 which should take 1hr 33mins, if the traffic allows. *Norman Rayfield/2RT2 group*

The Royal Forest Hotel in Rangers Road, Chingford is over one hundred years old. It was a bustling bus terminus for many years and, as can be seen below, London Transport provided its staff with a mobile canteen. This is one of the trailer canteen units towed into place by a Bedford tractor unit. An inspectors' hut is on the far right. The eight buses in this view are RTs 2020, 2072, 1583, 391, 3031, 4214, 2958 and RM 224. The date is 25th March 1967. *Mick Webber*

Stamford Hill lies on the site of the old Roman road Ermine Street which is now the A10, and has the largest community of Haredi Jews in Europe. K2 class trolleybus No 1226 has arrived from London Docks and will shortly do a U-turn and stand on the opposite side for its return trip. Its sister vehicle, 1218, is about to turn in front. The 647 was introduced in February 1939 to replace tram route 47, and it in turn will be replaced by new Routemasters in July 1961 on route 67, and an extension to existing route 47. The ornate Edwardian terrace in the background, happily survives. *Mick Webber Collection*

The Henley Arms is situated in Albert Road, Silvertown. King George V Dock was immediately to the north, and the railway lines to Custom House and Stratford to the south. An L3 class trolleybus on route 669 to Stratford picks up passengers at a request stop, as a steam locomotive on the right hauls a four coach train towards Silvertown. This line, to North Woolwich, was opened in June 1847 from Stratford. Steam disappeared in 1963 and the line was closed in 2006. The Docklands Light Railway now serves the area with a station at King George V. The trolleybuses were withdrawn by February 1960. The Moped OAN 73 is a German-built NSU 'Quickly', a 49cc machine of which over one million were sold between 1953 and 1963. *Fred Ivey*

In this view, we are looking up City Road northward with Old Street Underground station on the right. The trolleybus is L1 class 1358, which is fitted with coasting and run-back brakes for the steep Highgate Hill. Sister vehicle 1355 precedes it on the 615, and three Austin cars take centre stage at this busy junction where trolleybus wires cross for routes into Holborn to the left. It is 9th July 1960, and route 611 will be withdrawn on the 20th, and the 615 and 639 in the following February, although trolleybuses on routes 609 and 641 will continue late into 1961. The site is unrecognisable today, with a large roundabout at this point. *LTPS*

A busy entrance to Aldgate bus station. Buses, trolleybuses and Green Line coaches all used this point. The date is 24th September 1959 and the trolleybuses are being replaced in a programme that was to last until May 1962. An L3 class vehicle enters the bus station on the rush hour route 569, and the blind has already been set for its return to Poplar depot. In November it will be withdrawn with other routes in the area, and replaced by new Routemaster buses. The bus on the left is RTL 1310 which is leaving on route 26 for Leyton on a route introduced earlier in the trolleybus replacement programme to cover route 661. An RT in the background is on the 78; it will shortly cross Tower Bridge on its way to leafy Dulwich. *LTPS*

During the early years of the war, dockers in the Plaistow area were in need of extra trolleybuses to get them to work as the buses coming from the north were nearly always full when they reached here. This problem was addressed by January 1941, when a turning point was wired up via Bull Road, Willis Road and Holbrook Road. Trolleybuses showed 'Plaistow Station' on the blinds. K1 class 1278 has just turned into Bull Road from Plaistow Road to commence this turn, and will wait for time in Willis Road. Evidence of new post-war development can be seen on the right, this area being hard hit during the war owing to the close proximity to the Docks. A typical pram of the period can be seen with the once very familiar tricycle. *Fred Ivey*

Route 649A was a Sunday only route that commenced on 17th April 1949. Stamford Hill's K1 class No 1105 was a 1939 delivery and is seen here leaving Bruce Grove and joining the main High Road on its way south to Liverpool Street. The scene has not changed today, with Bruce Grove station just off to the left of the picture. The station opened in July 1872 as part of the Stoke Newington and Edmonton Railway. Trains here take passengers south into Liverpool Street, or Enfield and Cheshunt to the north. The station is now on the London Overground network. *Denis Battams/2RT2 Group*

The end of trolleybuses at stage 13 of the conversion scheme came on the night of January 2nd 1962. In the days prior to that, London was subjected to heavy snow, and keeping the buses running was a struggle. The trolleybus routes affected in this stage were the 645, 660, 662 and 666 running from Colindale, Finchley and Stonebridge depots. The 660, 662 and 666 all passed through Craven Park, and at this junction the 662 entered from the right. This unidentified L3 class trolleybus is working on the 660 to Hammersmith. *Mick Webber Collection*

North Finchley bus and trolleybus station New Year's Day 1962. The large building on the right is the Gaumont cinema. This 1,390 seater lavish picture palace was opened in July 1937, and occupied this large site until it was closed in October 1980 and demolished in 1987. RM 514 was new in October 1960 and is working from Highgate on route 17, which had replaced trolleybuses on routes 517 and 617 in February 1961. The trolleybus is N1 class No 1633 on route 660 to Hammersmith, which will also be replaced by new Routemasters in a couple of days, on new route 260. *Mick Webber Collection*

Kingsland High Street at the junction with Dalston Lane on the right. RM 752 was delivered in April 1961 and is on route 149, which replaced trolleybus 649 in July of the same year. This once busy trolleybus junction has seen its last electric vehicles, although some wiring remains in place. Catford garage's RT 3572 bound for Lewisham brings up the rear. High Street names once familiar, such as Meakers shirts and Sanders the jewellers have long gone, although Boots the chemist remains. A mark one Vauxhall Victor is followed by a flatbed TK Bedford, once one of the most common lorries on the road. *LTPS*

Opposite RM 941 was delivered in November 1961 to Wood Green for trolleybus replacement at stage 12 of the conversion scheme. This is London Wall, and the bus bears blinds for the new route 141 which replaced trolleybus 641, with a Monday to Friday southern extension beyond Moorgate to Grove Park. The bus may be on familiarisation trails, as there are staff in evidence on board. New building works can be seen in an area that was heavily bombed in the last war. *Sport & General*

The West India Docks consisted of three docks, the first two of which opened 1802. The southern dock of the three followed on in the 1860s. The access to these docks from the Thames, was straddled by a bascule bridge in Manchester Road. In 1967 the Port Authority, faced with a maintenance bill of some £200,000, decided that the bridge, which had been unreliable for some time, was not worth the expenditure and the decision was taken to replace it. RTL 183 on route 277 crosses the bridge on 2nd September 1967 on its way to Mildmay Park. The docks were closed in 1980. *Mick Webber*

Rotherhithe Tunnel was built between 1904 and 1908 at a cost of about £1m. The lanes are only just over 8ft wide and therefore all buses using it, and the tunnel at Blackwall, used tyres with reinforced walls to help stand up to the rubbing on the steel kerbs. Buses had very little room to pass each other and it was especially difficult negotiating the bends in the tunnels. Route 82 worked from Stepney East through the tunnel to Rotherhithe via a loop using Redriff Road. RTL 1457 enters the tunnel on the south side on 27th April 1968 and, as it is showing Blackwall Tunnel, is probably working back to its garage at Poplar. *Mick Webber*

Blackwall Lane, Greenwich on 25th May 1968. It is wet and overcast as RTL 1410 picks up passengers on its way to Bromley-by-Bow. Route 108 has been a tunnel route since March 1914. The mix of small shops on the right have now all gone, and the Barclays Bank on the corner is now an antiques shop. The building dominating the background is the Granada cinema. Its days of showing films was about to end in June, and the once part-time Bingo there was about to take over. It was opened by Gracie Fields in September 1937 and could seat nearly 2,000 people. In the first few years of the 21st Century it was converted to apartments and its appearance altered considerably. *Mick Webber*

It is 3rd December 1967 and work is under way to build the new southern approach road to Blackwall Tunnel. One of the many disruptive jobs to be carried out was the rebuilding of the railway bridge at the bottom of Westcombe Hill. Whilst this was being done, all bus routes were diverted via Halstow Road, and Humber Road. RTL 1499 from Poplar climbs the very steep Halstow Road on route 108A, and approaches a bridge over the railway. The houses on the left are all late Victorian, and are typical of the housing stock in the immediate area. Distant chimneys and gasometers will soon be a thing of the past. The 108A was a Mon-Fri rush hours and weekend route. *Mick Webber*

The 5C was a Saturday only route running between Becontree Heath and Bloomsbury. It was worked by Poplar using Routemasters, with short journeys operated by West Ham. Poplar's RM 138 is seen in Great Eastern Street, Shoreditch in the mid-1960s. The railway bridge in the background, long since demolished, carried the line from Broad Street to Dalston Junction, which closed in June 1986. This bus has one of the earlier production bodies, which were not fitted with upper deck front opening windows. The 5C was one of a small number of London Transport central area routes with C suffixes to be operated by Routemasters, others being the 77C, 81C, 90C and 130C. *Peter Mitchell*

The people of Lewisham were used to the River Quaggy overflowing into the High Street after heavy rain. One of those occasions was on 16th September 1968 and RT 2562 from Catford garage makes its way home through the water. The policeman is wearing his wellingtons as he supervises the traffic which includes two following RTs, a British Road Services AEC lorry and a Maidstone & District coach. The Duke of Cambridge pub had existed here in one form or another since 1858, the building here replacing the Victorian structure in the 1930s. The pub and the whole terrace behind on both sides, was demolished in 1987. Extensive work on the river defences has now consigned this type of event to history. *Mick Webber*

The main A2 at Deptford. Deptford High Street is to the left and Tanners Hill to the right. Deptford's claim to fame was that it was the first Royal Dockyard operating from the mid-16th to the late 19th century. The buildings on the right and left in this view all still stand but the distant building with the tower, which was Gardiners department store, has long gone. Route 177 was a tram replacement route that commenced on 6th July 1952, covering former tram routes 36 and 38. RT 689 heads for Blackfriars on 17th June 1967. *Mick Webber*

On 18th April 1966 new route 500, the first of the 'Red Arrow' routes, commenced. It worked from Victoria Station to Marble Arch during rush hours, and at other times worked a circular from Victoria via Hyde Park Corner, Hanover Square, Oxford Street, and back to Victoria. The vehicles chosen for this work were AECs with bodywork by Strachan's, designed to carry 73 passengers, 48 of them standing. It was the start of a network of routes based on central railway stations. In its first year, XMS 2 pauses at the stop at Marble Arch with the imposing Cumberland Hotel as a backdrop. *Mick Webber Collection*

The Reshaping London's Buses plan was published in 1966, and was to introduce huge changes to the bus network, with many short one-man routes based on local areas. The new Wood Green routes commenced in September 1968 and the Saturday only route W6 worked from Northumberland Park to Turnpike Lane Station. The new AEC Merlin with MCW bodywork was chosen as one of the new classes to work these new routes. MBS 53 entered service in September 1968, and leads an RM on the 67. It was withdrawn in September 1974. *Michael Beamish*

MB 336 was new in November 1968 and first worked from Southall garage. Here it is on driver familiarisation duty from Highgate garage as it passes RM 508 on the 143 at Hendon, a route that would soon be taken over by the new class. The unreliability of these new vehicles is well known, and this example lasted only until August 1975. *Michael Beamish*

New Red Arrow route 509 commenced on 27th October 1969 and this view was taken three days later in Cromwell Road, outside the Victoria and Albert Museum. It was a circular route from Victoria via Sloane Square, Albert Hall, and Knightsbridge. MBA 580 was delivered in September 1969 to Walworth. It is a rare sight to see this part of London virtually traffic-free. The route operated on Mondays to Fridays only. *Peter Mitchell*

Open land of 275 acres makes up Blackheath and the Roman road Watling Street crosses its wastes. Dick Turpin allegedly rode to York via Blackheath. Henry VI was met on the heath by the Mayor of London in 1431, and Henry VIII celebrated his meeting with Anne of Cleves here. It can still be a bit bleak in bad weather, and on the morning of 9th January 1968 the residents woke up to find a thick covering of snow. RT 1817, on the right, has slipped sideways on Prince Charles Road, and can't get any traction. The driver of RT 1727 had decided to try his luck on the pavement but still didn't get anywhere. The traffic on the main A2 in the background is moving slowly, but it will be a while before the rest of the roads are passable. *Mick Webber*